COPING
WHEN YOUR SPOUSE DIES

D0063928

COPING
WHEN YOUR SPOUSE DIES

MEDARD LAZ

FOREWORD BY EMELIA ALBERICO,
EXECUTIVE DIRECTOR OF THE BEGINNING EXPERIENCE

Liguori
ONE LIGUORI DRIVE
LIGUORI MO 63057-9999

Imprimi Potest:
Richard Thibodeau, CSsR
Provincial, Denver Province
The Redemptorists

Imprimatur:
Most Reverend Michael J. Sheridan
Auxiliary Bishop, Archdiocese of St. Louis

ISBN 978-0-7648-0226-3
Library of Congress Catalog Card Number: 98-65698
© 1998, Medard Laz
Printed in the United States of America
14 13 12 11 / 12 11 10 9

Scripture quotations are from the *New American Bible*, © 1970, by the
Confraternity of Christian Doctrine, Washington, D.C., and are used
by permission of copyright owner. All rights reserved.

This book was previously published under the title *Helps for the Widowed*, © 1983, Liguori Publications.

Liguori Publications, a nonprofit corporation, is an apostolate of the
Redemptorists. To learn more about the Redemptorist Congregation,
visit *Redemptorists.com*.

To order call, 800-325-9521
www.liguori.org

Cover design by Christine Kraus
Cover photo by Pat Roberts

CONTENTS

FOREWORD

The journey through pain is a solitary one, but traveling the path with a map can be a clearer, more defined way through the pain than journeying blindly. Following the pastoral road in this book will help both the newly widowed as well as those widowed for a longer period of time.

Many grieving people hold the illusion that the way to feeling better after a significant loss is endless and the way to being whole is beyond endless. For all of us who grieve, Father Medard Laz gives constructive ways of putting the pain behind. With his help we can identify the various stages of grief. Once we do this, we are gifted with the knowledge that the feelings experienced on this painful journey are normal.

The concrete examples given here by those who have experienced the trauma of being widowed are helpful signposts along the lonely journey. Med's pertinent questions after each chapter not only make the journey less fearful but also provide powerful tools that clearly define ways of healing.

This book, then, is the map that we who have lost a loved one have searched for in our desperate attempt to stop our agony. Med holds out his hand to help people in pain. He encourages us to stay with the pain through our jagged journey. By taking his hand and following the self-help steps in this book, we are able to reach beyond the darkness to new birth, hope, love, and peace.

Emelia Alberico,
Executive Director
The Beginning Experience

The Beginning Experience is an international peer ministry for separated, divorced, and widowed persons and their children. It is a process that facilitates the resolution of grief, promotes healing, and helps free people to live and love themselves, others, and God. The Beginning Experience Weekend is the foundation of the ministry, with support programs and outreach to youth as integral to the ministry. For more information on the Beginning Experience Weekend, contact the Beginning Experience International Ministry Center, 1657 Commerce Drive, South Bend, IN 46628; toll-free phone 866-610-8877; fax 574-283-0287; www.beginningexperience.org. E-mail us through the Contact Us page on our Web site.

INTRODUCTION

Death is a reality that few people care to talk about. When death strikes their spouse, they feel totally helpless. There are so many questions and so few answers—if any.

This book does not try to solve the problems that you face as a widow or widower, but it attempts to deal with the central issues that are present in your life after the death of your spouse. It is intended to provide support in your suffering, to make you aware that you are not isolated in what you are feeling. You are intimately involved in one of life's greatest mysteries, that of death and resurrection. You cannot bring back your spouse or the days of your marriage, but *you* can be resurrected to a new life.

You know that death and resurrection are basic to life. Both physically and spiritually, your emphasis must now be on resurrection. After you have experienced the agony caused by the death of your spouse, you may be tempted, for example, to withdraw from all social contacts. But this is not giving God or yourself a second chance.

This book will help you to *go through the pain* of the death and find resurrection or new life. You, of course, want to run from the pain and avoid the grief of your situation. The tendency is to bury your feelings rather than have others see you crying or depressed. In the long run this only leads to physical and emotional illness. Why bury your feelings or avoid expressing them? Going through the stages of your grief rather than steering clear of the agony will eventually help you to a new beginning in life. You will, in time, discover that rebirth is well worth the price of your pain.

By dealing primarily with feelings common to men and women, this book is intended for both widows and widowers. Its aim is to be a spiritual and an emotional support. As an individual, you can use it for personal healing; as a member of a small support group, you can utilize it as a resource book for your discussions.

To further aid you in the healing process, each chapter concludes with a set of questions. Your answers should be written down. In this way you will begin to see yourself more clearly, and you will provide yourself with definite data for your discussions with others.

A special note of thanks to those widows and widowers in the Beginning Experience who have shared their grief and their rebirth with me. They have made possible the telling of this Easter story.

1

LIFE IS CHANGED—NOT ENDED

❦

"I was not prepared. When I heard the word, 'dead,' my whole body went numb. This could not be happening to me."

No matter how sudden or forewarned, no matter your age, the depth of your faith, or your state in life—you are not prepared for the shock and the finality of the death of your spouse. You cannot anticipate the emotional trauma that his or her death brings to you. You seem so helplessly alone, even though many people are there to lend you support. Grief is your constant companion. Your whole being quakes with fear and disbelief. Nothing and no one can miraculously take away your suffering. You must go through it step-by-step, heartache by heartache.

Why? Why? Why? pounds away constantly in your head like an air hammer. You search for answers. From first grade on, you have been programmed toward finding answers. Death—its unanswered questions and resulting void—has no

answers. Death is and always will be a mystery. It will never
be solved until you yourself can look back at life from the
eternal beyond. Now, you will always see "through a glass
darkly," for human eyes are able to see no further.

When your spouse dies, it is tantamount to taking a
thousand-piece jigsaw puzzle, throwing it into the air, and
having the pieces land everywhere. The death of your spouse
reduces your life to scattered pieces. With the devastation you
feel, it will take months just to find and get the four corners
of your life back into place. Every piece, every aspect of
your life needs to be reexamined.

Your main difficulty in figuring out where all the pieces fit
is that there is no picture to guide you. With a regular jigsaw
puzzle there is a picture on the box to let you see what you
are assembling. You can collect complementary colors and
shapes to aid in the piecing together. Death has no color or
shape. There is no picture to guide your work; the pieces
themselves are empty and blank. You are not sure what your
new life is supposed to look like. In many respects, you don't
care; your pain is so great.

One reason for all of this is *shattered dreams.* The most
shocking aspect of the death of your spouse is that there
are no more tomorrows for the two of you; no horizons to
plan or to talk about over coffee. Arguments and difficulties
were often overcome because there was hope in tomorrow.
Without another day, where is the hope?

So much of your marriage hinged on those dreams of

tomorrow. Dreams made permanent commitments possible. "Once the children are gone...." "After the home is paid off...." "When we go to Hawaii...." "Once I retire...." These were all such shining hopes which made your days seem less troublesome than they were. Take away the dreams and the one person with whom you have shared them, and life has little or no meaning.

In losing your spouse, you have a built-in sense of being cut off. You have to decide who God is calling you to be toward the middle or the end of your life—a struggle similar to that in your earlier years. God is always calling you toward a deeper life, a richer knowledge of yourself. He never beckons you into self-pity or self-indulgence, into total grieving or licking your wounds in life. God is calling you to the acceptance of your pain as glory, to death as birth, to a greater expectancy of what life means to you and who *you are still becoming.* This is never-ending, because it goes even beyond the grave into a new resurrected life.

On your journey through the early stages of one of life's darkest experiences, there are four things you can do to help yourself: (1) accept the reality; (2) express your emotions; (3) find support in others; and (4) keep a journal.

ACCEPT REALITY

Facing the finality of death brings on an emotional tidal wave. Whether an illness of years prepared you for the moment or the death was totally unexpected—you went into shock when death arrived. You have never been more alone than at the time of the announcement. *Why me? What have either of us done to deserve this? Gone...gone!...I'll never make it alone...gone!* The words hit you like a fast-moving train. With your head, your heart, and your whole being pounding, you are lucky to be breathing, to be alive yourself.

As much as you try to fight the finality of death's call, the arrangements that need to be made quickly bring your senses back to a partial awareness. Before you lies the stark reality— the body. In order to lay your spouse to rest you must enter a new world: the funeral director, choice of a coffin, cemetery lot, flowers, wake, arrival of your family, clothes for the body, stream of mourners, the death notice, informing relatives and friends, wishers of sympathy, prayers, condolences, services at church, eulogy, closing of the coffin, funeral procession, hearse, pallbearers, the cemetery, funeral luncheon, the thank-you cards. For a lifetime all of these have been so foreign to your vocabulary, so distant from your mind.

Decisions. Decisions. You are expected to make more meaningful decisions in half a day than you have made in half a lifetime. You make them because you are forced to do so. Considering your shock and your numbness, you decide as best you can. You cannot run and hide. Hour by hour you realize that this is not all a bad dream from which you can wake yourself. You must accept the reality of your loved one's death. From the very first time as a child when you experienced a loss or a death, you knew that you would someday go through it again with a loved one. There is nothing you can do to bring your spouse back. You cannot change the past.

What you can do is place yourself, your spouse, and your whole family in God's hands. Our destinies always rest in the hands of others; but as long as they are in God's hands, and we are the ones who put them there, God's plan for us will be carried out no matter what turn life takes.

Hold on tightly to the deepest roots of your faith. Your faith cannot be centered on the dead past. You know that death and resurrection go hand in hand. As you are now forced to accept death, so also accept the reality of the resurrection. Ours is a God of death and resurrection.

If we have been united with [Christ] through likeness to his death, so shall we be through a like resurrection (Romans 6:5).

The Preface of the Mass for the Dead says it well:

The sadness of death gives way to the bright promise of immortality. Lord, for your faithful people life is changed, not ended. When the body of our earthly dwelling lies in death we gain an everlasting dwelling place in heaven.

Do not stop with the bodily image of your spouse. Go on to fashion an image of his or her newly liberated soul. Do not stop with the death; move on to thoughts of resurrection. Eventually, these thoughts will find a home in your heart, where the Lord needs to dwell and live in order to give you hope, peace, and comfort. Do not bury the body of your spouse without accepting resurrection in return.

Express Your Emotions

Everyone expresses his or her emotions to life's greatest hurts differently. You may be torn with uncontrollable crying or become extremely sullen. You may carry on with your limitless "Whys" or you may withdraw from others.

Remember that, with the death of your spouse, you were mortally wounded, too. As an emotional blow, it is second to none. On occasion you must open your wounds and let your emotions out—whatever they are. This is the only way that you will be healed. The time, the place, and the frequency are all up to you. We are all different and there is no set pattern in dealing with death.

But do not keep bandages on your wounds for too long, saying to yourself that you have to always be strong and not break down for the sake of the children or the family. God gave you two shoulders to carry your crosses. He also gave you the shoulders of others so that you can cry on them when the need arises. You do not have to be strong all of the time.

When death forces you to unwrap your love, you find pain, anger, and loneliness. Do not be afraid to mourn openly.

"The whole world is going about its business and I'm in another world—hell!"

"The worst part is reaching out at night in bed and finding no one there."

"I've been doing better for weeks. Then I vacuumed the rug and the cord got stuck on a leg of the sofa. I looked behind me for my husband to hold the cord as he always did, but he was not there. I sat down and cried."

Jesus expressed his feelings openly at the death of his friend, Lazarus:

> When Mary came to the place where Jesus was, seeing him, she fell at his feet and said to him, "Lord, if you had been here my brother would never have died." When Jesus saw her weeping, and the Jews who had accompanied her also weeping, he was troubled in spirit, moved by the deepest emotions. "Where have you laid him?" he asked. "Lord, come and see," they said. Jesus began to weep, which caused the Jews to remark, "See how much he loved him!" (John 11:32-36).

Find Support in Others

When your spouse died, you were surrounded by people—family, relatives, neighbors, friends, coworkers, clergypersons, etc. You could hardly be alone with so many people around you. No matter their promises, the passage of time sent them all back to their usual routines; and you were left with your daily life—but now without that one special person who gave meaning and purpose to so much of your life. Your loneliness seems terminal. It is so easy to get caught up in yourself, to be a martyr and to not want to bother anyone. "No one cares. They have their own lives to lead."

You have to reach out and continue to make overtures to others. This may be as new an experience as the death was. Your marriage was of its very nature protective. You may never have had to depend on others like you must do now. But never consider yourself a burden. You are not a burden but a blessing. Doing for others is not the only way of being a Christian. You can allow others to practice their Christianity by helping you in your need. "I hate to depend on others to drive me, but they seem to enjoy doing it."

Your neighbors, friends, and coworkers can help you to keep some perspective in your life. They can encourage you to stay in touch with the larger world that still does exist.

When your daily routine resumes, try to be with those who can accept and understand your emotions. You do not need people around you who continually say, "Don't worry, you will be all right" *(when you are not all right)* or those who keep repeating, "I'm sorry" or "You poor thing."

If it is bedtime and you are depressed and feeling alone, call a family member or a friend with whom you can share what you are feeling. Remember that tears cannot be seen over the telephone, so call. People do care. You are not a bother. YOU must take the initiative. It is very healing to be with family and friends who will recall the many happy times that you and your spouse had with them. You have a storehouse of joyful memories to share with those who care.

We all need to be needed. Make yourself useful. Family, friends, and neighbors all could use someone to put up shelves, help hang the drapes, pick up something from the store, go to the post office, or clean out a basement or a garage. As Anne Frank wrote in her diary, "No one ever became poor by giving." Being useful gives you a sense of worth and this can help you over the rough spots, especially the Saturdays and the Sundays, the loneliest days of the week. Death entered your life without your control. Now the only thing in your control is your own life.

KEEP A JOURNAL

Many times there will be no one around with whom to share; and even if there is, you may not feel like talking. Writing down your feelings can be most helpful. You want to keep in touch with who you are throughout this ordeal and, more especially, who you are becoming. You want to keep in touch with the feelings that accompany the movement of your life from death to a new life.

Keeping a journal is not the same as keeping a diary. You are not recording merely what happened but how you are feeling and why you are feeling that way. You need to be in contact with the ups and downs, so that the direction and the flow of your life becomes more evident.

Each day try to record significant events of that day and how you felt. Record the milestones and the millstones. Some days you may write whole paragraphs, other days it may be one event and one feeling—"Slept!"—"Heavenly!"

You deserve a record of your journey back to life. You experience many mood swings with much depression. It is easy to forget where you have been and where you are. One mental storm can practically sink the progress that you have made. You want to enshrine the milestones—a good night's sleep, your weekend away, and your first day back at work. These are the steppingstones to your new life.

If writing, especially the writing of feelings, is difficult for you, try the "hot pen" method. Just keep writing whatever comes into your head. Don't stop; don't worry about the lines making sense, about the spelling, or even about making sentences. The goal is to get down on paper what is inside of you. Over weeks and months you will be able to gauge your journey and your progress. Occasional slips will seem less like sliding down the Alps when you can visually retrace your steps through your journal. You will be able to view the change in your emotional patterns.

Get a notebook that will be special to you, one with lots

of paper. Find a time of day that is convenient for you, or write whenever you feel the need to write. And do not write just when you are down; those times are only a part of your journey. Take time to sort out what you have written.

Talk to God in your journal. Make it personal; God should be a close friend of yours. Write God a letter. Later when you reread it, God will talk to you. He will show you how at times he has carried you, and through it all how you have made it.

When you answer the questions at the close of this and the following chapters, write the responses in your journal. Writing helps you to reflect on your words as they are put on paper. It gives form and expression to the feelings inside you. You will find yourself expressing feelings you were not even aware you had. Writing helps you see inside yourself.

You may have a special friend who responds to you with empathy and whose words encourage you to focus on your feelings. You may choose to share what you have written with such a friend.

If you are part of a support group, these questions lend themselves to both writing and sharing in a group. But be sure the emphasis is on sharing feelings to provide mutual support and not on making judgments to reach inadequate solutions.

QUESTIONS

1. What emotions have you felt throughout your grieving period? List at least ten of them and write down the time or the events when you felt them.

2. What are some of your shattered dreams and how do you feel about them?

3. With whom do you find sharing your deeper self the easiest? the hardest?

4. What have been the milestones and the millstones in your journey to a new life? How do you feel about each of these?

5. Write a personal letter to God.

2

WORKING THROUGH YOUR GRIEF

Grief, sorrow, and loss are part of life; and there has never been a human life, the life of Jesus included, that has not experienced deep hurt attendant to loss and death.

As normal as grief is to your life, so also is getting stuck in your grief very normal. It is like the helplessness of driving your car in the ice and snow and getting stuck. You desperately want to get going, but the more you step on the gas pedal, the more the wheels keep spinning, digging the car in deeper. The same is true after your spouse dies. Because there was nothing that you could do to prevent the death of your spouse, you were helpless. You could not hold back the inevitable. In your helplessness you may well try to bury your grief and your anger. By doing so, however, you are only "spinning the wheels" of your emotions. Your grief is only being covered up, not dissolved.

Feelings that are buried alive come back, even years later,

to haunt you. They do not go away when they are buried or suppressed; they remain alive and can cause you great depression. You have no choice but to grieve. You must deal with your inner feelings of grief, express them, resolve them. To be healed, you need to identify the stages of your grief and, *passing through them,* arrive at a new life.

In her book *On Death and Dying,* Elisabeth Kübler-Ross speaks of five stages of grief that are present in the face of death: (1) denial, (2) anger, (3) bargaining, (4) resignation, (5) acceptance. If the death of your spouse was not sudden he or she experienced these stages in some order or fashion possibly getting caught up in one stage or another. You and other family members also went through and are still going through these stages.

It is important to remember that these stages are *normal* to loss and death. Everyone *should* go through them. You are not losing your mind because of the way you feel. It is essential to *pass through* these stages in whatever order you choose so that you do not keep on burying your feelings and your hurts. You will have to pass through them many, many times, because your wound is deep and your marriage lasted for a long time. It is OK to feel like you do at each stage; but remember, you are *passing through.* All of the grieving stages that you go through are ultimately healing.

DENIAL

The first stage is that of DENIAL: "No, this is not really happening to me." You do not want to believe that tragedy has struck you through the death of your spouse. No doubt during your marriage you rarely, if ever, talked about death, other than insurance arrangements or choice of burial plots.

If there was any illness attendant on the death, denial was probably there most of the time. You listened only to good reports from the doctor; you waited for a new wonder drug to use or a miracle to happen; or you simply lived for the good days when your spouse was feeling better, as you tried to hide the real condition. If this has been your case history, then denial may still be with you now. You refuse to say that your spouse has *died;* instead, you speak of him or her as having *passed away.* At some point, you need to enunciate the word *died,* no matter what emotions or tears come with it. Talking about the death over and over to family and friends at the wake beside the coffin is most trying, but the repetition does allow for the reality to sink in.

The countless changes and confrontations following the death touch you deeply—receiving bills and letters addressed "Mr. and Mrs.," signing cards for birthdays and holidays with only your name, handling your checks with both of your names on them and wondering about taking off one name, visiting the lawyer, turning your wedding ring around and around while telling yourself that you will never take it off your finger. All of these challenge you to deny what has happened. Your psyche is not ready to say "goodbye" or to begin a new life. For months you wait for your partner to walk in the door or to call you on the phone. Someone goes by who resembles your departed spouse and your heart skips, "It must be him/her." Death is just too final.

One course that denial takes is wearing an "I'm OK" mask. With it you try to show everyone that you are doing much better and that you will be fine from now on. Inside you may be dying a thousand deaths, but you never let on to anyone. You may well pride yourself on being the "perfect widow" or the "perfect widower"—in charge of your emotions and your life, being strong when you must be.

It is difficult to talk about death because we have to come to terms with it within ourselves before we can get beyond denial and share with others. Denial tries to short-circuit the hurt—to just talk or listen and not deal with the emotions.

Much of denial centers on your not wanting to let go of the deceased. It is quite normal to go to the cemetery frequently—several times a week or every weekend. It is not normal to avoid the cemetery at all costs. There is a certain benefit in being close to the remains—to look back, to have at least one-way communication, and to be surrounded by the reality of the many dead who are buried nearby. But if your visit becomes a compulsion, a routine that cannot be broken under any circumstances whatsoever, then denial has reached its limits.

Denial is normal. You and everyone else must go through it, but you cannot stay at denial for many months or bury your feelings of denial too deeply within.

ANGER

The second stage in your grief process is ANGER: "Why me? What did my spouse or I ever do to deserve this?" Murderers, embezzlers, prostitutes, thieves, and criminals populate the world in large numbers and they are doing well, while your partner is dead and you are at wits end.

You feel angry, but you are often helpless in your anger. You are angry with God, even with your spouse who left you, and you cannot understand how that can be. Sometimes your anger may be directed against others whom you felt were responsible for the death in some way, but again, you are helpless. You cannot bring your spouse back to life no matter how much you flare up.

Our society makes it difficult for you to voice your feelings. "Keep your chin up! Be strong! Or if you must, display your grief in the privacy of your own home." This is what society usually expects, but the anger that you feel will not go away by itself.

Perhaps you remain at the denial stage because you have been taught not to manifest your anger. "I'd rather not think about the many years he smoked more than two packs of cigarettes a day and the coughing fits he had each morning."

"She did such a fine job in raising the kids that I can't bring myself to admit that she is no longer here. But she did make them very dependent on her; and here I am left with four kids that I feel very incapable of raising."

To display anger over the way life has gone awry is not abnormal; it is a healing part of your journey back to life. If your anger is not allowed a healthy expression, it may fix itself on the wrong parties—yourself, the children, your parents, or others.

It is normal to be angry with God. The prophets in the Old Testament were. Of itself, anger is not a sign of disrespect. "Why God, why? How could you allow this to happen if you are a good God?" Neither God nor God's master plan is at fault; we just don't see things from his perspective. God created the human condition; we are creatures of body and soul. He does not protect our bodies from deterioration or death, nor does he prevent us from committing sins or having accidents. As we grope for understanding, critical of why God allows tragedies to happen, it is normal to have feelings of anger against him.

It is OK to feel anger against your deceased partner: "Why weren't you more careful on that icy road?" "Do you realize the mess you left me?" "Why did you insist on shoveling snow that wintry day? If you hadn't, you'd still be here."

You can best deal with your anger by sharing it with a counselor, a clergyperson, or a friend. In doing so, you can acquire an understanding of the anger.

The important consideration here is that you handle your anger in a *constructive* way. Rather than say, "I'll show you" or "I'll show everybody," you should be willing to say, "I'll show myself...that I can face the problems that death has brought and still be very much alive."

It is essential that you search out people who, while understanding your anger, will also check out your excesses. "You're going to have to stop talking about the doctor like that." The kind of person you do not need is one who placates you. "Don't worry, in a year you will have everything under control." Allow your anger to dissolve into tears. Water makes everything else in the world grow. Surely your tears will also help you to grow.

BARGAINING

BARGAINING is the third stage in the grief process.

"If only he had retired a few years earlier...."
"If only she had gone for regular checkups...."
"If only the cancer had been detected sooner...."
"If only he or she could have been strong enough to
   have surgery...."

The list is endless; and the "If onlys" prey upon your mind night and day as you try to convince yourself that there must have been some way of saving the life of your spouse and avoiding the agony you are now going through. You try to discover some means of bringing him or her back. But no matter what you do, death is a fact that cannot be undone.

There is no guarantee that an earlier retirement would have saved the life of your spouse.

✳ Regular checkups might have helped, but you cannot know whether what ultimately caused death would have been diagnosed at the time.

✳ You have no assurance that had the cancer been detected at an earlier stage your spouse would still be alive.

And if your spouse had been strong enough for surgery, you have no way of knowing whether the operation would have been successful.

There are few guarantees in life, and none of us can check off the date on the calendar when we want to die. Life and death are the result of many uncontrollable forces. We cannot add a second to the schedule planned for our arriving at the gates of eternity.

During the dying period you may have tried to bargain with God. "If God will only let my spouse live, I'll do... (anything)." Such prayers are worthwhile, yet they are said in desperation. You hoped for a miracle. It is not that God did not hear you or that God wanted the death to occur. God permits suffering and death so that there might be a greater experience of life—both in heaven and on earth. Besides, overindulgence in prayers of petition leaves little room for prayers of thanksgiving, praise, resignation, or forgiveness.

Praying in this one-sided fashion may have been your attempt to circumvent the hurt—the inner death and anguish with which you were struggling. If, instead, you ask God for help in bearing the cross of the death, you will not be tempted to blame God for failing to work a miracle.

RESIGNATION

The fourth step in the grief process is that of RESIGNATION: "Yes, me; this has all happened to me." The wishing and the hoping that this was all a bad dream begins to disappear. Resignation is difficult to reach; and even when attained, it is easily abandoned for one of the earlier steps. If you have not adequately lived through the earlier stages, resignation can quickly become depression as you turn those bitter and helpless feelings upon yourself.

When you begin to see yourself as widowed and unable to bring your spouse back, you will no longer feel set apart from the rest of the world. You will be able to pick up the pieces of your old routine, sort out your life, and begin to fit both the old and the new pieces into place.

Be prepared for many changes in your moods; you may go through a part of your day feeling joyful and buoyant—thoughts of the death rarely cross your mind. Then, from out of the blue, a word, a thought, or an event will strike you, and you will be back in the doldrums, feeling guilty for being happy, telling yourself that you should be sad and not happy.

It is often a tug of war with your emotional ups and downs. Be sure to make notes in your journal, describing the happy and the sad feelings, what prompted them and what changed them. With this you will be better able to hold on to the pleasant feelings and not let guilt steal them away.

When you start to take charge of your new life and your emotions, you must do so without allowing the circumstances of life to knock you off-balance. Your goal at this stage is to keep an even keel as you are tossed about. You have been weathering a terrible storm. Your most important task is to stay afloat.

Usually, several sessions with a counselor or a clergyperson can get you over the severe humps when you have little or no desire to go on living yourself. Eventually, you will learn how to *pick yourself up* from such depression. As time goes on, this will happen more readily. "There was a wedding in the family and I went to the church and the reception. I was doing fine and enjoyed the dinner. When the dancing started, my eyes kept filling up and I left early. Nevertheless, I was proud of myself for how well I had done."

Acceptance

The fifth and final step in the grief process is ACCEPTANCE. "Yes, this all happened to me and I'm doing fine." You have reached the acceptance stage when you no longer dwell on all the unfinished business of the past or worry continually about the uncertainty of the future. Rather, you live and enjoy the present moment with contentment. You do not hide your feelings; you express them willingly. You have reached acceptance when your sentences or thoughts are not prefaced with: "He/she always used to...." You make decisions without first asking yourself: "What would my wife/husband have done?" You have confidence in yourself, and you see yourself as a whole person and not as one-half of a couple.

When you look at your marriage, try not to idealize it. If, in fact, your marriage was better than most, then be grateful. But do not put either the marriage or your spouse on a pedestal. This will only make living today next to impossible. This does not mean that you should then dwell on the hard times. Acceptance means, rather, accepting the whole marriage—the bad and the good. There is no emotional benefit in idealizing what you had, no matter how happy you were.

If you felt that you could have had a much better marriage and that much was lacking in you and/or your spouse, then accept yourself, your spouse, and your marriage for what it was—very human. No one can be good and kind and loving all of the time. We all let each other down, some of us more than others. Try to remember your spouse as a *real* person, possessing both good qualities and bad.

You reach acceptance when you begin to live your own personal history. You make new friends; you stop relying solely on your family and on your old friends. You are willing to venture forth with life on your own, doing new things and exploring new places. Your "perfect widow/widower" mask has been laid aside.

Being lonely at times is not the worst fate in the world. You had many lonely moments while you were married. The acceptance stage is usually a long time in coming. There still will be lonely moments and even lonely days. A fuller acceptance and healing can take as long as five years. It will eventually arrive if you are willing to *pass through* these normal stages of your grief.

Remember that these grief stages do not always follow one another chronologically. You may experience denial and bargaining at the same time; you may go from acceptance back to anger; you may be at resignation over several aspects of the death but at denial or anger over other aspects.

These stages will recur from time to time and not necessarily in the same order. You may arrive at acceptance— really feeling that you are your old self again—only to uncover a letter your spouse had written you years ago, and you are pushed back to the earlier stages of grief. In writing down your feelings in your journal, try to identify the stage where you are. Write from your heart and not from your head. Pray that your return to one of the earlier stages, even though very severe and traumatic, will not be as long-lasting as the previous one.

For spiritual help, meditate on Jesus' Agony in the Garden as found in Matthew 26, Mark 14, and Luke 22. Jesus, too, went through the stages of grief:

Then he began to be filled with fear and distress. He said to them, "My heart is filled with sorrow to the point of death. Remain here and stay awake" (Mark 14:34).

DENIAL

He kept saying, *"Abba* (O Father), you have the power to do all things. Take this cup away from me (Mark 14:36).

ANGER

When he returned to his disciples, he found them asleep. He said to Peter, "So you could not stay awake with me for even an hour?" (Matthew 26:40).

BARGAINING

"My Father, if it is possible, let this cup pass me by" (Matthew 26:39).

RESIGNATION

"...yet not my will but yours be done." An angel then appeared to him from heaven to strengthen him. In his anguish he prayed with all the greater intensity, and his

sweat became like drops of blood falling to the ground
(Luke 22:42-44).

ACCEPTANCE

"Do you not suppose I can call on my Father to provide
at a moment's notice more than twelve legions of angels?
But then how would the Scriptures be fulfilled which
say it must happen this way?" (Matthew 26:53-54).

Jesus *passed through* agony, grief, and death at the age of
thirty-three in order to arrive at new life and Resurrection.
So can you.

QUESTIONS

1. Describe where you have been and are now at each of the
   five stages of grief and what you have felt at each stage.
2. Describe other significant losses in your life and how
   you went through the five stages and what your feelings
   were.
3. List some of the ways you acted in an attempt to hold on
   to your deceased spouse.
4. How have you worked at handling your anger in a constructive way?
5. Describe your mood changes, your emotional ups and
   downs. What prompted them and what changed them?

3
WHAT ABOUT
THE CHILDREN?

W hile it is difficult enough for adults to cope with death, it is almost impossible for children to comprehend. In order to talk adequately to your children about death, you must come to terms with it yourself. Hurting side by side with the children, going through the motions, and even trying to be overly kind are not sufficient. Your children must be allowed to share in the grief in their own way.

Because of all the pain that you have been going through, you may not be fully aware of what your children are experiencing internally. They may feel "...totally lost in a strange, dark room" or they may say, "Life is a complete bummer" or "I'll never be happy again, no matter how long I live." Simply because they are silent or are not crying does not mean that things have settled down inside of them. It is also false to assume that because you are doing better, reaching the acceptance stage, your children must also be doing better.

The reactions children have to death can be varied—from silent to noisy, from overindulging to not eating, from daydreaming to being totally practical, from hostility to meekness. A common reaction is one of fear—of almost everything: the dark, noises in the night, simple ailments, moving to another home, other losses, etc.

Your children, whether young or in their teens, cannot receive enough reassurances that everything will be all right. They need to be made to feel secure, and you are the primary person to do this. Sitting on the bed until they fall asleep and giving them multiple hugs and caresses—this is what is needed to help ease the pain. Your children should never have to ask for this continued contact and reassurance; you should give it spontaneously. A closeness, never before experienced between parent and children, should be forthcoming for many, many months.

Comments like "Be brave," "Be strong," or "You're the man/woman in the family now" are often made to the children without your knowledge. These only result in harm. Most of all, let your children be children. Of course, this does not imply irresponsibility. "You have to be brave to cry" may well be what your children need to hear. Regular dialogue sessions with them and frequent reassurances are most necessary.

The Five Stages

Just as you go through the five stages of grief described in the previous chapter, so do your children also go through them in their own way.

The DENIAL stage is usually in evidence because your children cannot grasp the finality of death. They fantasize that this is all a bad dream and that the missing parent will eventually return home. At first they refuse to believe that this has happened, especially if they have had little exposure to loss or death. It is a mistake to tell younger children that the parent is merely asleep in the coffin. "Don't worry. Daddy's all right. He's just sleeping." When your children perceive you as distraught, weepy or sullen, instead of asking why, they may withdraw further into a shell of denial.

The ANGER stage can manifest itself in any number of ways. Your children may be involved in fights; or they may have little or no desire to concentrate or study, the result being a drop in grades. They may lash out at you, blaming you for the death, for not having been a better spouse or seeing that their parent had better care. Since you are the one closest to them, you bear the brunt of their anger. They may refuse to eat, study, or accept discipline. They are acting out the way they feel. Remember, all this is normal.

Many of their remarks may come out in an angry fashion. It is not you with whom they are angry, but when they are at a loss to blame someone, you are that someone. They may be angry with God for having taken their parent, and so may refuse to go to church. Try to listen to your children and hear the hurt. Be understanding and talk it out. Let them put their anger into words, assuring them that it is OK to be upset with God. Tell them their parent is safe with God. Assure them over and over that one day their sadness will slowly begin to leave and the family will be happy again.

Your children may repress their anger and refuse to cry because they see you crying or looking upset. They do not want to add to your misery. They think they are helping you by repressing their own emotions. Let them know that it is all right to cry. Do everything humanly possible to draw them out to talk and open up.

BARGAINING is natural for children who have lost a parent. Because of guilt feelings, it is not uncommon for children to feel in some way responsible for the death. If the death was not sudden, the children have probably struck many a bargain with God. "If you let my Daddy live, I'll clean my room every day." "If my Mom gets well, I'll eat my spinach and do my homework without anyone saying a word." You must spend tender time with your children, letting them know that God heard their prayer but still wanted the missing spouse to be in a happier home in heaven. So that this joy can be a reality, the tears and the sorrow must be borne by the family.

Also keep in mind the fact that children often believe things happen because they wish them. In an angry moment, they may have wished their parent dead. Continue to reassure your children that everyone does this without thinking and this had nothing to do with the death.

RESIGNATION will begin to happen when the emotional level settles down and the children realize that the departed parent is not going to return home again. As order and tranquillity are reestablished in the home and new patterns of daily living are set up for eating, getting to school, and visiting friends after school, the children become resigned to this new life. Their prayers have not been answered, but they realize that life does go on—for the family and for themselves.

"Life isn't fair." This is what the children often may be feeling, even though they may or may not express it verbally. You must take the time to explain that, in fact, life is not always fair, that no one can have his or her parents or loved ones forever. Then assure them that this does not mean that the family cannot be happy again. Say to them: "Life isn't fair, but we can work together to make it brighter."

Children reach the ACCEPTANCE stage when they realize that they are not the only ones in the world who have lost a parent through death, divorce, or separation. In some schools or classrooms as many as fifty percent of the children are living with only one parent. This is not a case of misery loving company but of recognition of the children's identity and receiving needed support. They are adjusting to the fact that they are not the only ones in the world coming from a single-parent home. In time their scars will heal. At birthdays, graduations, Christmastime, and other special days, they will particularly feel the loss. More and more, however, they will recognize that they have *their own lives* to lead and that this is of the utmost importance.

"At first, all I could visualize were the many problems in our family without a father around. Now I realize that we are still a family, and we do many things as a family. I wish Dad were still with us, but he and God made other plans that could not include us."

TEN POINTS TO REMEMBER

In summary, here are ten simple points for you to remember in dealing with your children after the death of your spouse:

1. Death is a mystery. We will never fully understand why a loved one had to die. We can take comfort in the fact that Jesus died for us and was resurrected to life. We put our faith and our hope in Jesus.
2. The parent is safe with God. Tragic or painful deaths can cause the children long-lasting wounds. They want to know: "Where is Daddy?" or "Where is Mommy?" Here is where you can put your own faith into both action and words. Concretize the warmth, happiness, love, and joy that your spouse is enjoying. Though this is painful, it will

help you and your children in the healing process. Do it often.

3. Talk about the happy times of the past. Let the children know that life will be full of joyous times in the future. The deceased wants the family to smile and to be happy more than anything else.

4. No one is really to blame. Anger accomplishes nothing. Forgiving is difficult but necessary. God's invitation, written in crooked lines, arrived; and the parent had to go home to God.

5. The death was not a punishment. God did not look and see what you were doing and then punish the family. Rather he saw that it was time to end the life here on earth and begin another for the parent.

6. You need each other in the family. Hugs and kisses are great helps. Ask for a back rub and give one without asking. Work on making the other family members feel special—with treats, flowers, or a simple "I love you."

7. Crying is OK. In fact, it is more than OK. "Come on, dear, get it all out. It's all right." (And where does it say that you have to be strong for family members and not cry?) Crying helps the soul to heal.

8. Make every effort to be together with your children. Remain close to them, though try not to cling. Go for walks. Tuck them in at night or sit on the bed and talk. Try to be there when they return home after school.

9. Pray together at meals and at bedtime. Try spontaneous

prayer. Make the prayers ones of thanksgiving and joy rather than formal ones that ask only for things.

10.Get the children to talk out their feelings. Encourage them by revealing your own feelings. Do not let days or weeks slip by without trying to get them out of their shell. Try a variety of leading but gentle statements and questions. "I miss him, too." "What time of day is worst for you?" Such remarks are better than: "Is everything OK?" Your children need space, but do not let them live in outer space.

These suggestions are offered because you need quality time with your children more than ever. Added work, worries, and responsibilities may give the children the impression that both parents are gone—one to God, the other to work and grief.

Given your continued love and attention, no permanent scars or effects are likely to stay with your children. If anything, they will become even more adept at handling crises and life's uncertainties than children coming from homes where both parents are still living. There is more than one way to define the word *family*.

QUESTIONS

1. How do you feel about discussing the death of your spouse with your children?

2. How have you tried to reassure your children and make them feel more secure since the death of your spouse?

3. Describe how your children are weathering the five grief stages. What stages have they gone through and where are they now?

4. Make your own list of five or ten simple points to remember in dealing with your children after the death of your spouse.

5. Write a personal letter to each of your children, expressing your support, your love, and your dreams for them.

4
WHAT TO DO
ABOUT GUILT FEELINGS

Death forces you to look back over the ups and downs of your marriage. In doing so, it is easy to see how, if you had to do it all over again, you would have acted differently.

"I wish I had been a better wife/husband." In a word, going back over the marriage in your mind can cause you deep feelings of *guilt,* even in the best of marriages. The list of SHOULD HAVES can be lengthy.

I SHOULD HAVE

…been more affectionate.

…kept my mouth shut more often.

…remembered anniversaries and special days with cards and flowers.

…not been so wrapped up in work or the kids.

…made a point of doing more together.

…spent more money on my spouse.

…traveled more.

…not teased or been so critical.

…been more patient and not so angry or hostile at times.

…been more loving and not so quiet or withdrawn.

Such a list of guilt feelings can become quite overwhelming. Like grief, guilt can eat away inside of you; and it, too, needs to be resolved. Guilt ensues from the past because you cannot go back in time and say, "I'm sorry" or "I love you." The earthly part of the relationship is ended. The past can be examined and dealt with but not changed. All that can be changed is the present.

The unfair part of being *the* survivor is that you are the one left behind to handle all the affairs, deal with all the problems, and shoulder all the guilt. You have to carry the entire load of the rights and especially the wrongs. You *both* did things that were wrong in the marriage, but there is only you left to worry, fret, and feel the guilt.

Your fights, disagreements, and misunderstandings all had two sides to them; now there is only one side—your side—left to resolve the guilt.

"Why did I hound him about all the sports programs he watched on TV?"

"Why was fixing up the house so important to me all of the time?"

"Why did I stop for a drink when I should have come home sooner after work?"

"She was not asking for the world when she wanted me to go shopping with her, yet I rarely went."

Quite possibly your spouse was at times married to the TV set, and the house was in dire need of repair. On occasion you may have needed that drink after work, and going shopping was not your strong suit. This is said not to ration-alize your guilt feelings but to allow for the other side of the story, which you usually presented well. Now, however, there is no one left to hear the case, so the guilt is all yours.

Psychologically and spiritually, it is therapeutic to sort out your life and your guilt. Writing about it in your journal can be helpful. Once guilt is exposed, you can deal with it and your life can go forward. But in doing so, it is necessary to distinguish between *realistic* guilt and *unrealistic* guilt, so as not to make yourself solely responsible for all of the hurts, the inconsistencies, etc. of the marriage.

REALISTIC GUILT

Realistic guilt results from what you actually said or did during your marriage and after the death of your spouse. You are responsible for your words and deeds—abusiveness, drinking bouts, coldness, cheating, profanity, and so on. There are no excuses. There is no pretending otherwise. You feel guilty about what you actually did or said. Unless resolved or forgiven, this guilt can be present and gnaw away at you for years like a spiritual cancer. It can put a halt to any true spiritual growth.

Because it is real guilt, it can be admitted, dealt with, and forgiven. But admission of realistic guilt is often difficult because it makes you assess yourself; it forces you to stop pretending or running. Once you admit your guilt, you are ready to do the following:

FORGIVE YOURSELF. Admit to yourself that you are human and weak, that you make mistakes and that you, too, are a sinner. Avoiding guilt means taking it out on yourself: "How could anyone love or even like me?" Forgiving yourself means unplugging the logjams of the past here in the present: "I was wrong, totally wrong, and this hurts me, my spouse, and my family. I hate what I did, but I truly love ME, the sinner. The logjam was caused because I did not love myself, because I did not like what I said or did. By fully admitting my wrongdoing to myself, I can start loving me again.

ASK FORGIVENESS OF OTHERS. Through prayer and with tears, ask forgiveness of your departed spouse. Though dead, he or she is still capable of forgiving you. The inner peace that you experience will be the sign of forgiveness. Ask forgiveness of your children and others. A tremendous inner healing will result.

SEEK FORGIVENESS FROM GOD. This can be done with the help of a priest or minister. A Catholic has the sacrament of reconciliation available as a tangible sign of God's healing power. This sacrament gives the assurance of God's acceptance of you, your love, and your sincere sorrow.

Seeking forgiveness from self, others, and God is a surefire way of resolving your realistic guilt so as to be a whole and fully alive person.

UNREALISTIC GUILT

Unrealistic guilt results from situations which you did not cause or were only *partially* responsible for:

"Why didn't I make my spouse go to the doctor sooner?"
"Why didn't I show my love more often?"
"Why did I always highlight our money problems?"
"Why did I continually complain about the house being messy?"

You can get carried away with such thoughts. Remember that your spouse was an adult. He or she also had to be responsible, and many events that happened were beyond the control of both of you. In marriage, healthcare still depends very much on the individual; no one is perfect in his or her display of love and affection; money worries *were a* major concern; and the house *was* often in disarray.

Most of us have a tendency to be hard on ourselves, to heap blame and guilt on ourselves for everything that goes wrong in a given situation. Few of us recognize that if we fail to be all we can be at home or we do not show or tell others that they are loved today we may not have the opportunity to do so tomorrow. And when one of those others is our departed spouse, we drown in a sea of guilt.

Unrealistic guilt should be banished from your life. Yet you continue to blame yourself for past events—even though you were not responsible for them. "If only I had been there when he/she died." It is impossible to always be with someone. The fact that you were not there for whatever reason is not a clear cause for guilt. That is why the guilt you are shouldering is unrealistic.

Attempting to live with unrealistic guilt is life-defeating. It is like trying to have a picnic without food. Many of your actions after the death of your spouse are laden with unrealistic guilt. If you go to Hawaii, you feel guilty because he or she wanted to go but never got the chance. If you sell the house, you feel guilty about disposing of his or her treasured possessions. If you have some fun and laughter, you feel guilty because you should still be mourning and not be happy.

Everyone lives with tinges of guilt. If you have reached the acceptance stage described in chapter two, you can set unrealistic guilt aside. You can live your present life fully, as you see fit, no longer being compelled always to meas-ure what you are doing against the memory of your departed spouse.

Closely related to unrealistic guilt are regrets. It is a

natural tendency for you to regret the times you did not say: "I love you" or "You're so special to me." Likewise, you regret all that you neglected to do—helping with household projects or helping with the business or the children. It is a rare person who can honestly say. "I have no regrets."

You must learn to balance your regrets with your successes and accomplishments, with all that was so very good about your relationship. Hopefully, you will be able to echo the sentiments of Paul Anka's song in which he sings about having a few regrets but they're too few to mention.

Placing a halo on your deceased partner also contributes to your unrealistic guilt. "When I lost him/her, I lost the very best." "God threw away the mold after God created him/her." There is the tendency to canonize the deceased, to look at only one side of his or her personality.

You can also build up unrealistic guilt by going to the opposite extreme: always thinking ill of your spouse or looking only at his or her faults. Do not be afraid to sort through *all* of your thoughts and feelings—the positive and the negative. But be realistic. Try not to make the deceased bigger or smaller than life. If you find yourself eulogizing your spouse, give yourself a good pat on the back as well, because you are not so bad either.

It is most helpful to use your journal to write down your realistic and unrealistic guilts. Once you see your realistic guilts on paper, you can learn to forgive yourself; you can seek forgiveness from your departed spouse and from God.

And when you examine your unrealistic guilts, seeing them for what they really are, you can more easily determine how to rid yourself of them.

Examine the following inventory.

A List of Unrealistic Guilts

- Using the life insurance money to buy things and to make my life more enjoyable.
- Blaming myself for the emotional ups and downs of the children.
- Not missing my spouse as much as I think I should.
- Disposing of his or her clothes and keepsakes.
- Taking off my wedding ring.
- All of the regrets:
  — having wished him or her ill, even dead, in the past.
  — praying that my spouse would die, even if it were to ease his or her pain.
  — for not having told my spouse that his or her illness was terminal (if it was).
  — for not having made the marriage happier.
  — for having been so wrapped up in my job and in material things.
  — for not having been more caring and supportive at the end.
  — for not saying, "I love you," more often at the end.

A List of Realistic Guilts

- I so often upset my family with my temper and my lack of patience.
- I teased unmercifully and was jealous without reason.
- I used alcohol and drugs to excess.
- I neglected my spouse and the children to take care of my own needs.
- I resented her love for her own family.
- I was not responsive to my spouse and the children.
- I took out my own anger and frustration on the children and other family members by screaming at them and by demanding too much.
- I dwelt constantly on the past.

Once you have finished your two lists, deal first with your unrealistic guilt. Be sure that you have made a complete list of your regrets. Banish them from your life.

Then take your list of realistic guilt and add the following words wherever they can be inserted: "*I was wrong... I am sorry...I forgive myself...I pray that he/she will forgive me...I beg God's forgiveness.*" Here is how it would look:

"I was wrong in upsetting others with my temper and my lack of patience. I am sorry that I made everyone suffer because of me. I forgive myself for having slammed doors and broken dishes. I pray that my spouse and my family will forgive me for the misery I caused them. I beg God's forgiveness for being less than what he made me to be."

Do this for each of your realistic guilts. This way you will own your guilt and you will thereby resolve it.

QUESTIONS

1. Make a list of all the SHOULD HAVES as you review your marriage. Label each as realistic or unrealistic guilt.
2. What realistic and unrealistic guilts are you particularly harboring? How do you feel about each?
3. What do you find most difficult about forgiving yourself?
4. How have you been particularly hard on yourself throughout your grieving?
5. How have you placed a halo on your deceased spouse?

5
HANDLING
SPECIAL DAYS

A nother difficult consequence of surviving the death of your spouse is having to cope with the holidays and other special days—Christmas, New Year's, Easter, Valentine's Day, Mother's Day, Father's Day, Thanksgiving, birthdays, and anniversaries. There is no way that you can delete these days from your calendar, no matter how big an eraser you have.

The days and the seasons are etched into your calendar and your future. The gifts, the tree, and the cards at Christmas, the hearts on Valentine's Day, the turkey at Thanksgiving, the remembrance of birthdays, and the wedding ring at anniversary time—all these intensify the ache you feel inside. You may try to explain away your pain, even flush it out with your tears, in an attempt to make it disappear. If this does not work, you may try to block the person and the past out of your mind as though he or she never existed.

Of course, none of this works, and you are left holding the holiday bag.

You must remind yourself that another four and a half billion people on the earth have survived a loss similar to yours. They, too, felt sure that they could not survive. But they have lived through it, and their experience can give you the reassurance that the burden of the holidays, birthdays, and anniversaries does become easier. The load does lighten as time passes. Many of the people around you are also suffering the agony of a personal loss, although they do not share or communicate this. They, too, are not overjoyed that Christmas or one of the other holidays is here.

Live and Love Today

As you look back on the years of your marriage, you can easily see how quickly time passed. So much was here and then quickly gone. What does this tell you? Take the time to ponder. Life is short. We possess no one, save the Lord, forever. The lesson: You have others in your life right now. Make every possible effort to enjoy the fleeting temporariness of your life with them. Do not hold back your love out of fear. Love, care, and share while you still have each other. Let them presume nothing of your love. Spell it out through words and deeds.

But once you have made your journey into the past through your memories and you return to your present life, never expect your life today to be the same as it was in the past or to bring you similar satisfaction. You are just learning to crawl and to walk again; you are starting a new way of life alone. This is your chance to really live today, so don't ruin it by saying over and over, "It's not the same."

PLAN AHEAD

As you approach the holidays or a special day, you must do so using both your head and your heart. You should be prepared for the new emotional implications of the season or the day. Try to plan, as best you can, how you are going to act or react to what will be happening. You must decide:

(1) Which traditions of the past are good so that you can continue them;

(2) Which traditions you want to leave in the past;

(3) Which good traditions can be done in a different way.

You must find the courage to let go of certain traditions or, at least, do certain ones differently. Writing in your journal will again be helpful. For example:

Christmastime

1. Traditions to continue: having the children, the grandchildren, and the family over for dinner; sending out the Christmas cards; decorating the house, and putting up the Christmas tree.

2. Traditions to discontinue: giving to public Christmas funds (but continuing your private charities); listening endlessly to Christmas carols played on radio or record player; having *numerous* family gatherings at the house.

3. Traditions to do differently: going to church services, but not at midnight; giving Christmas cookies, but not homemade ones; decorating the outside of the house, but having the children do it.

New Year's Day

1. Traditions to continue: watching the Rose Bowl parade.

2. Traditions to discontinue: having the New Year's Day brunch at the house.

3. Traditions to do differently: ringing in the New Year, but at home with your children and not in public with married friends.

His or Her Birthday Anniversary

1. Traditions to continue: having the family over for dinner.
2. Traditions to discontinue: making or ordering a special birthday cake.
3. Traditions to do differently: preparing the house for the occasion, but deliberately refusing to add those little touches that he or she was so fond of.

You must make every effort to hold on to the important traditions and not go into a shell or build walls around yourself. Some traditions need to be dropped for your own emotional stability. Others can be maintained, but in a different way. Your journal can help you to plan and plot your way through the holidays and the other special days that can be emotionally difficult.

SET PRIORITIES

In handling these special days, it is necessary to set priorities. As a grieving person you are not able to function at your usual optimum. You can only deal with so much at one time. In your journal, set short-range as well as long-range goals for yourself. Your short-range goal may simply be "to get through this afternoon or this evening." Your long-range goal may be the gradual acceptance of your spouse's death, the constant effort to overcome your sadness, and the ceaseless endeavor to make life meaningful again.

In setting your priorities for the holidays, focus on the things that are most important to you. "I really wanted to have the whole family over, and I did. The living room needed painting and everything was not spic and span, but I didn't let this bother me." The things that are not important need to be seen as such, and then put aside or laid to rest. "Every year we ran from one party to the next, never asking why. This year I am happy to be with my immediate family."

GROW IN FAITH

Lastly, deepen your faith. Allow the holidays and the other special days to transform your inner life now and to add deeper roots to your beliefs. Spend time contemplating the inner meaning of the holidays or a particular day from the past. Each day and season has a spiritual dimension that can add to your inner tranquillity and peace, but you must make the effort.

"For months all I did was ask myself over and over, Why?… Why?…Why? I dreaded the Easter holidays, but on Good Friday afternoon I went to church and spent some time reading the Bible. I made the Stations of the Cross and gazed at Christ hanging there. I could still hear all of my 'whys' in the background, but now I was asking 'why?' about the Savior of the world and all that he endured with his suffering and death. My spouse is at least laid to rest; Jesus is still on the cross at church. In my own life I decided to take Jesus down from the cross. That was a great step for me. And my next step was to place myself there in his stead. On Easter Sunday not only did the sun shine, a smile broke through the clouds of my pain for the first time in many months."

"As I blew out the candles on my birthday cake, I sensed how easily a year, or even an entire lifetime, can be extinguished. Thinking about this in bed that night, I decided to light a candle to replace the one I blew out. I determined to stop at a nursing home and read to the elderly, and I made plans to take my granddaughter out to dinner on her eighteenth birthday."

"With Christmas coming, I've read over the story of the birth of Jesus on several occasions. Each time I do so, another word or phrase embeds itself in my mind: 'no room'… 'tidings of great joy'…'laid him in a manger'…'Mary treas-ured all these things and reflected on them in her heart.'"

Your journal entries and your private reflections will add a new dimension to your life. With God's help and the strength of your faith you can begin to fill the void that death left behind.

You will have many questions to ask about life, death, suffering, God, and eternal life. This is a good sign. Find a sympathetic friend or clergyman or a support group, and spend some time in talking about these topics. And listen to the Lord in the meantime.

To help you through this most trying time, pray and meditate frequently on the Serenity Prayer:

God, grant me
the serenity to accept the things I cannot change,
the courage to change the things I can,
and the wisdom to know the difference.

As a result of struggling through the holidays and other special days, you will be a stronger person and surely a better person than you were when you turned the pages of the calendar with a shaking hand and a pounding heart.

QUESTIONS

1. How can you make every moment count with those who are important in your life right now?
2. Compose a litany of beautiful memories and describe in a word or a phrase how each of these makes you feel.
3. List a number of areas in your life where you have been telling yourself, "It's not the same," and then write down what you hope to do about each of them.
4. What are the priorities in your life at present? What are your long-range and your short-range goals?
5. Choose a holiday or a special day and describe how its spiritual dimension adds to your personal faith.

6
FINDING GOD
IN YOUR LIFE

W hen God seems far away, who moved?" These words, inscribed on plaques and banners, speak a penetrating truth: God may seem distant from us, especially during or after a crisis, but he has not hidden himself from us; rather, we have clouded our own vision.

Death challenges you to look ever so deeply at your life. You begin to view your existence from a different vantage point, seeing God thoroughly entwined with everything that happens to you. In death, God not only draws your spouse's spirit close, but God also uncovers the reality of the other side of life to you—the spiritual and the everlasting.

Stay in touch with the spirit of your deceased spouse. Death has not destroyed the spiritual bond between the two of you; for it is usually through death that we receive deeper insights into exactly who that person was, what motivated him or her. We come to the fullest knowledge of the other only after death. This was true of Jesus—as we read in the accounts of his life and death—and it is certainly true of your departed spouse. Death and resurrection place before you the true value of the person whom you married. And, with the passing of your spouse, you can also see more clearly the value of your own life.

ACCEPT YOUR NEW LIFE

Do not become frightened of death. Absorb it with the eyes of faith so that a whole new surge of God's love can engulf and transform your goals and your dreams. The heart of your life's desires is still there, still attainable. Not having dinner for two each night does not mean that you are doomed to having dinner by yourself for the rest of your life. Keep the door open. Be courageous and set an extra place or two for others in your life.

As recommended in the last chapter, you are beginning to live your traditions differently now, because you have been to the grave and you have come back, not a loser or a solitary soul but a new person with a new mission in life. You are now a witness to death and to the overcoming of death through resurrection.

God gives you all that you need for your journey—your enlightened self, your family, friends, your Church, the Scriptures, etc. Remember, too, that the people, the opportunities, and the graces ever present in your life are meant

to be utilized. Don't brush them aside with the excuse that
you are not ready to accept your new life.

"I've come to find that God has answered my prayers. For
a time I thought I heard him saying, *'No,'* especially when
my spouse departed this life. Now I realize that God was
saying *'Yes,' 'Yes,' 'Yes,'* to me and to my spouse in a very
soft and gentle way."

Death is an affirmation of life. We live to die. We die to
live—eternally.

COME TO KNOW GOD

Ours is not a punishing, distant, or noncaring God. God
is Someone who is involved in the very heartbeat of life and
death. God sent us his only Son to be born, to live, to suffer
and die. Like your spouse, Jesus died and then rose to new
life. No one, not even the Son of God, was destined to call
earth home forever.

You find God most evident in the mysteries of birth, life,
suffering, and death. The greater the mystery, the more you
find God. To have a continually lingering *"Why?"* in your
mind or on your tongue is not necessarily an unhealthy
situation. Yours can be a *Why* of discernment—even as
you once asked why you were chosen to be a parent or why
you were given a certain job to do. Here on earth, you will
never know the reasons. Nor are you really doubting when
you ask, *"Why?"* You are believing; for life is not a problem

to be solved but a mystery to be lived and shared, to be lost and found.

Read the parable of the Prodigal Son and note that it should more aptly be named the Loving Father; for the father, not the son, is the central figure in the story. Come to know and believe in God as your loving Father. God calls you back to life, to once again celebrate life.

You may have gone astray like the prodigal, not deserving to be called *son* or *daughter*. Your loving Father waits patiently for you to return. And when you do, God forgives you and cherishes you more than ever.

Or you may be like the other brother in the story. You have done your duty. You have toed the line all your life; yet death stared you in the face and stole your loved one. And you cried out, "Why, Lord?" Now you see the loving Father beckoning you to come celebrate, for the one who was dead has come back to life, the one who was lost is now found.

Come to know and believe in Jesus as your suffering, dying, and rising Savior. On the cross, it seemed he had nothing left to give, but listen to his words: "Woman, there is your son....There is your mother" (John 19:26-27). How could he do this? *He* was her son, not John. She was *his* mother. Yet Jesus gave away even that close, intimate relationship which he shared with Mary. Death is a time for giving one's all, one's closest and dearest of loves. Jesus entrusted his mother and John into each other's safekeeping. You must give your spouse to the Lord, entrust your spouse into his hands.

Only a few days after his death, the risen Jesus would say to those who mourned his passing, "Feed my lambs.... Feed my sheep" (John 21:15,17). "Go into the whole world and proclaim the good news to all creation" (Mark 16:15). As the Lord urged his disciples, so he urges you not to sit back but to go forward with life. In your case, however, he prompts you to listen to the good news, because right now you especially need to be comforted by it and to be fed with the justice, holiness, and peace that it brings.

Come to know and believe in the Holy Spirit as the breath of God's continuing love ever present within you. For Jesus has promised:

> I will not leave you orphaned;...
> the Paraclete, the Holy Spirit
> whom the Father will send in my name,
> will instruct you in everything...(John 14:18,26).

The death of your spouse has caused the light of love within you to flicker, but it has not gone out. It has become more intense and penetrating. The void, the emptiness, the soul-rending loss and pain can only be healed with the gentle touch of the Spirit of God. The sum and substance of your life lies locked deep *within you,* not in a grave, not in an apartment or a house. Where the pain is most intense is where the mystery of love is most real.

The Spirit gives you no aspirin or tranquilizer but deep inner peace and serenity. The Spirit unchains you; the Spirit heals, and recreates a new heart within you. The Spirit does not do this instantaneously. Step by step, by human trial and error, the Spirit moves you toward your destiny in this world and fulfillment in heaven. God acts in your life so well that you do not even realize how hard at work God is.

CONTACT GOD THROUGH PRAYER

Your prayers bring you into contact with the Father, the Son, and the Holy Spirit. Your prayers should not only be those of petition but also of praise, thanksgiving, and sorrow. In your present situation, you have probably worn out every form of petition prayers. Begin now to include the other forms as well:

PRAISE. "Lord, you are wonderful! My family is so supportive. The minute I start going downhill, you send someone special to help pick me up."

THANKSGIVING. "Thank you, Lord, for allowing me to be the one whose life has continued on in this world. I do have a lot going for myself and a whole lot to give to others."

SORROW. "Lord, I'm sorry for all of the guilty sentences that I've passed on myself and others. I'm sorry for not listening more clearly to your words."

At prayer, you face yourself as you really are and you discover God when you open yourself to the Spirit. When you are alone like this, God's Spirit is as near to you as you are to yourself. To pray to God is really no more than to look at God and let God look at you; and in that mutual exchange you begin to see life, love, and eternity. In this intimate, personal conversation with God, you need not utter a single word; you absorb rather than chatter or worry.

You listen with your heart. This is the only way to know what God is saying to you. You begin to feel free as your spouse is free, you begin to feel safe as your spouse is safe; and, like your spouse who is truly at rest, you begin to feel at rest for the first time in many months.

For you are free, safe, and at rest in the Lord, and only God can give you these precious gifts.

Only in God be at rest, my soul,
for from him comes my hope (Psalm 62:6).

QUESTIONS

1. Since the death of your beloved, what fuller knowledge have you discovered about your spouse, yourself, and God?
2. In what way has God helped you to face your day-by-day life?
3. How do you identify with the prodigal son, the other brother, and the loving father in the parable?
4. Write short prayers of praise, thanksgiving, and sorrow to God.
5. Describe how you feel when you listen to God with your heart.

7

NEW HORIZONS

ⵣ

There comes a point in your present life when you will have to make a most difficult decision—whether to go on *living* or to simply go on *existing*. Some months after the funeral, you begin to question your responses to all the stand-ard questions: "How are you doing?" "Oh, better." *Better than what?* "Is there anything that we can do?" "No, not really." *What can anyone do?* This is the time when you must choose to live or to be numbered amongst the living dead. You reach a point where you must let go of your spouse and let him or her rest in peace.

When you dispose of your spouse's clothing and per-sonal belongings, you are letting go. When you become bored with telling the same old stories and start talking about your life today, you are letting go. When you take a vacation or at least a short trip to get out of the house, you are letting go. You reach acceptance when your wounds are healed and you decide not to look at the scars any longer.

You are the one who must decide not to wait for the next unfortunate event to happen which will reopen old, but still sensitive, wounds. You must take control of your own life, your own destiny. It is only after you let go of your departed spouse and your past marriage that you can begin to form a new identity for yourself.

Your whole being resists this, because generally, you enjoyed your old identity as a married person, and you resent your present state of widowhood. You feel like a leper. Surviving the death was trauma enough; forming a new identity for yourself is asking a lot. But you *can* make a new beginning.

DEVELOP TRUST AND CONFIDENCE

It is easy to back away from others ("They don't understand." "Nobody really cares.") because of a lack of trust in yourself. The death of your spouse has shattered your ego, your very self. Remember the nursery rhyme:

Humpty Dumpty sat on a wall.
Humpty Dumpty had a great fall.
All the king's horses and all the king's men
Could not put Humpty Dumpty back together again.

So true. After all that has befallen you, only you can put yourself back together again.

As a result of the death, you tend to mistrust your own judgment, having depended on your spouse for so many matters. "I'm so confused about what to do. Should I sell the car or hold on to it? Should I take this part-time job? Should I go to the neighbor's party or not?"

During your marriage you made many choices that you truly believed were valid and good; but now, after the death, you begin to wonder. And, as a result, you lack confidence in your present decisions about life. This hesitancy comes from that deep inner feeling of loss: "My marriage is over; therefore, my life has no future."

Uncover the many qualities that your spouse helped you to develop, and use them as building blocks to start a new life. You will discover that you are both intelligent and strong: you can sort out bills and rearrange the furniture. You are independent: you can go shopping alone and show up at family functions unescorted. You are understanding—when your lawyer says he is busy or when your children fail to call at reasonable intervals. You are sympathetic—to a neighbor whose father recently fell sick and to an acquaintance who just lost his job. You are determined—when the automatic washer, the coffee maker, and the TV all break down at the same time you hang in there and go for help. You are patient—with the door-to-door salesman and with the boy next door who is a day overdue in coming to mow your lawn.

During your marriage, you may not have noticed you had

these qualities because your spouse took care of the situations when it was needed. But these are the gifts from your spouse that endure even after he or she is gone.

You have many hidden resources and strengths to tap. God gave you all the tools you need, not only to survive but also to overcome the gloomiest aspects of your present state in life. Only one person in the world can defeat you, and that is you yourself.

When you are in harmony with yourself, with your own interior life, then you are in harmony with those around you. And if you are in harmony with God, you are able to take the disjointed parts of your life and fit them together more easily. With your established long-range goal in mind, you move one step at a time in fulfilling your short-range goals. And in that process you derive a deep sense of belonging, of living your own life instead of being carried along by it.

RECOGNIZE THAT OTHERS CARE

Whenever you relapse into loneliness and depression, you ask: "Does anybody care about me? Does anybody *really* care about me?" The caring of others truly does exist, but you may have to look for it, even reach out for it. Maybe your initial "poor me" attitude caused others to withdraw. Family and friends may not be sure whether their calls, visits, and offers of help are intruding or really helping. If you desire a caring love in your life once again, you may well have to go and search for it. You are never too old to go out looking. Nor is your vision ever too clouded to recognize and respond to an expression of caring love, however veiled it may be.

- You receive an invitation to a party where other widowed persons will be in attendance. *Somebody cares!*
- A friend phones just to say, "Hello." *Somebody cares!*
- A dinner invitation comes from your children. *Somebody cares!*
- A clergyperson stops to ask how you feel and how you are doing. *Somebody cares!*
- A lawyer gives you additional time and service and does not charge you extra. *Somebody cares!*
- A doctor spends an extra fifteen minutes advising you to relax and heal your inner self. *Somebody cares!*
- A stranger at the cemetery cuts the grass or brings water for your flowers. *Somebody cares!*
- A member of the opposite sex is genuinely interested in you and not just interested in playing games. *Somebody cares!*
- An acquaintance makes a firm offer to help with your income tax. *Somebody cares!*
- A note of tribute to you and your spouse arrives from a coworker. *Somebody cares!*

Some of this caring will easily come your way. At other times you will have to search for it. But always be ready to receive it. Take each situation as it is intended—as an act of caring, an act of love.

To feel important again, you may have to get a job or find volunteer work. Most of your life you were on the giving end of things—on the job or at home, immediately after the funeral you were on the receiving end. But don't allow that to continue for long; it will only add to your depression and loneliness. A paycheck, the assurance of a job well done, the nodding assent of a sick patient, or the joy radiant in the eyes of children makes you feel that life is once again flowing in your veins.

Regulate Your Sexual Life

To become emotionally close to a member of the opposite sex, even after much time has passed, may be difficult for you. An emotional and spiritual bond still exists between you and your spouse. To have strong feelings for another person and to go out socially can shore up many guilty feelings. Again, you must travel at your own pace.

For many months you will not want a member of the opposite sex to touch you, even on the dance floor, because your internal hurt is so bad. The tendency is to avoid getting involved, although some try to bury the past and their feelings very quickly and start dating within a couple of months. This can be devastating in the end, since it takes several years to adequately work through one's grief.

What you need most of all from others at this time is the *caring* love that was described earlier. This is known as unconditional love. It creates no dependencies. It has no strings attached. Caring love is a personal response to the genuine worth of the other.

In seeking this caring love from friends you will have to make some adjustments in your sexual life. Sex was always integral to your marriage; it unified, healed and sustained you. Now you will be tempted to vacillate between two extremes. On the one hand, you may want to avoid encounters with members of the opposite sex because they are too painful to your wounded self. You tell yourself and others that you are a one-love-of-a-lifetime person. On the other hand, you may become obsessed with sex. It can prey on your mind almost constantly, although you are not even trying to seek out a caring-love relationship.

You may well venture to ask yourself: "How can I live without sex after years of having it in my marriage?" But before you can answer that question, you must ask yourself another: "Am I ready to love again?" This can be further defined by asking yourself: "Am I ready to trust another, to give myself completely and unconditionally? Am I willing to commit myself to another person? Am I whole and complete in myself or am I looking for someone else to make me happy? Am I only looking for companionship? Am I ready to care about one, single person again?" If the answer to any of the above questions is "No," or there is hesitation or the need for qualification, then you are only playing games with sex, no matter what your age might be or how you try to rationalize your needs or boast about your maturity. Under these circumstances, sex soon becomes a form of usury.

Your sexual feelings are extremely powerful; they are as strong as any that you possess, and the death of your spouse in no way lessens them. But just as in marriage you had to control them—when your spouse was ill or absent or when it was the wrong time—so now you must learn to discipline yourself.

If you do not receive caring love, you will tend to become lonely. But loneliness is not the worst feeling in the world. Everyone gets lonely, from the pope in the Vatican to the widow or widower on a fixed income. You are not alone. Think back to how lonely you felt even on the happiest days of your marriage. In your journal check out for yourself the why of your present loneliness. Is it the holiday season or an anniversary? Is it self-pity that you are feeling? Are you afraid of being alone? Are you terrified of facing the future? Once you discover the reason (your written journal will help you here), you may be able to respond to your loneliness in a way other than by sexual fantasy or sexual encounter.

"The dances and the clubs where I went seeking companionship all turned me off. When I got involved in my parish I found that I could care again. I still get lonely. But I've found a friend with whom I can share my ups and downs, and just having such a friend makes for a lot fewer downs. My friend does care."

Your goal is to reach a point where you can be alone without being lonely. You will come to enjoy and savor your aloneness with the peace and tranquillity it brings you. Your loneliness will be a void that you will learn to fill with new friends and old, with experiences that you never knew existed in your world. Your new life will eventually mean more time alone to bloom and grow, rather than more lonely time to brood and pine away.

QUESTIONS

1. Describe why you want to go on living. How do you feel about what you have written?
2. What are some of the ways that you have already let go of the past?
3. Write a "Thank you" letter to your deceased spouse.
4. List the personal qualities your spouse helped you to develop and which you can especially use in your present state.
5. How do you feel about becoming emotionally close to a member of the opposite sex?

ABOUT THE AUTHOR

A s a priest, self-help speaker, author, founder of several support groups, and founding board member of the Beginning Experience, Medard Laz has helped thousands of people worldwide deal with a multitude of issues, ranging from marriage to the death of a loved one. He has written nine books, including *Life After the Divorce, Making Parish Meetings Work,* and the best-selling *Love Adds a Little Chocolate: 100 Stories to Brighten Your Day and Sweeten Your Life.*